Gold Star Favorites

Level Two

Compiled and arranged by Wesley Schaum

CD orchestrations by Jeff Schaum

FOREWORD

This series offers students an appealing variety of styles in a single album. A brief paragraph of background information is provided for most pieces. Folk music includes spirituals. Jazz styles include boogie, blues, ragtime, swing and rock.

All books include a CD with orchestrated accompaniments. Each piece has two tracks: 1) Performance tempo. 2) Practice tempo. An optional duet accompaniment, which fits in with the orchestration, is included for some of the pieces.

The intent of the CD is to provide an incentive for practice by demonstrating how the finished piece will sound. The slower practice tempo assists the student in maintaining a steady beat, using the correct rhythm and gaining valuable ensemble experience while making practice more fun.

> A performance /practice CD is enclosed in an envelope attached to the back inside cover.

INDEX

Schaum Publications, Inc.
10235 N. Port Washington Rd. • Mequon, WI 53092
www.schaumpiano.net

03-62
KS-1

Entertainer

Moderato ♩ = 108-120

Scott Joplin

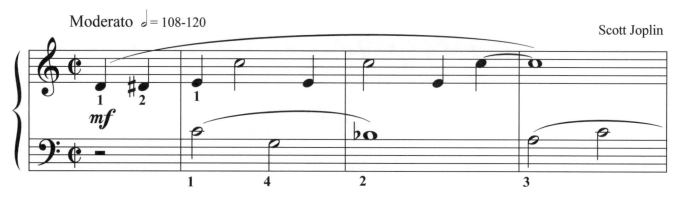

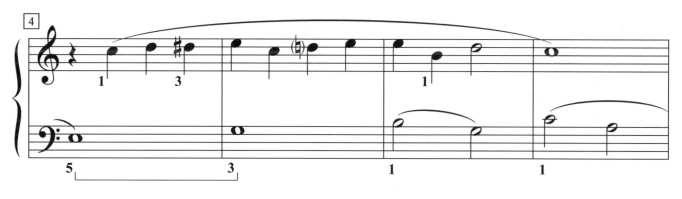

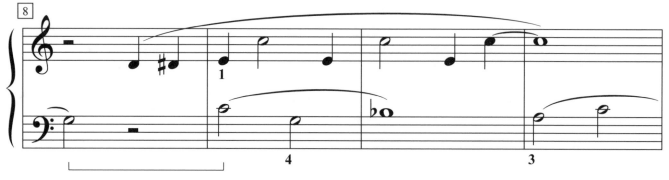

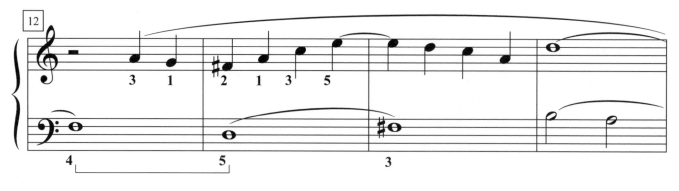

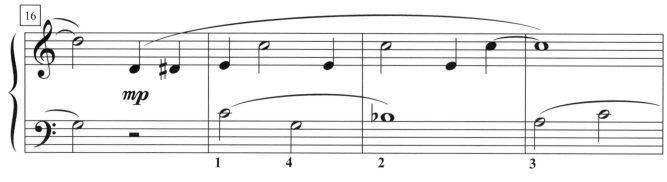

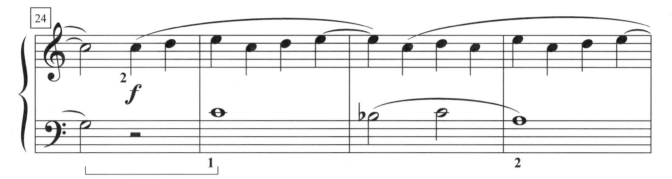

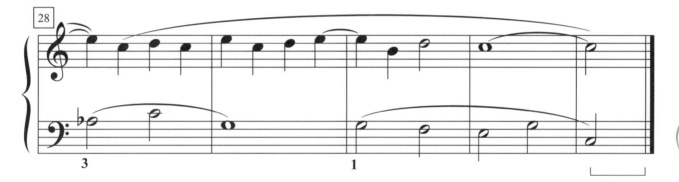

Scott Joplin was born near Texarkana, Texas in 1868. He is the best known African-American composer of ragtime music. During his lifetime he achieved fame as a performing pianist, teacher and composer. He lived until 1917. Although Joplin is most famous for his ragtime piano works, he also composed two operas, a ballet and a small number of songs, waltzes and marches. "The Entertainer" is the best known among dozens of ragtime pieces which he wrote. Another of his compositions, "Peacherine Rag," is included in this book.

CD Track 1: Performance tempo
CD Track 2: Practice tempo (played twice)
(Each track includes two-measure introduction)

Scarborough Fair

Tranquillo ♩ = 104-112

English Folk Song

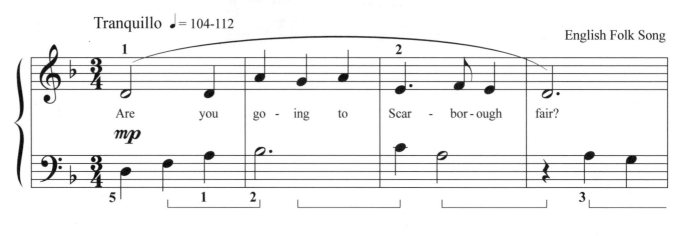

Are you go-ing to Scar-bor-ough fair?

mp

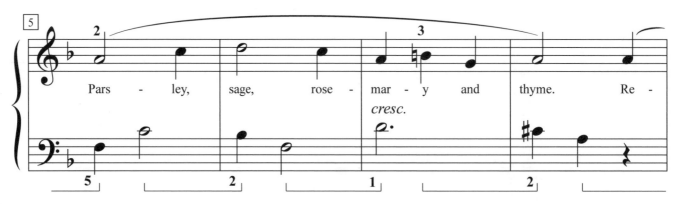

Pars-ley, sage, rose-mar-y and thyme. Re-

cresc.

mem-ber me to one who lives there, For

f

once she was a true love of mine.

dim.   mp

CD Track 3: Performance tempo
CD Track 4: Practice tempo (played twice)

Wearing of the Green

Giocoso ♩ = 84-96

Irish Folk Song

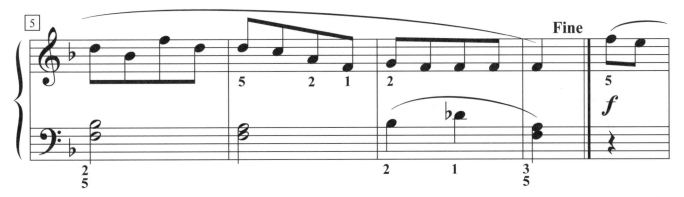

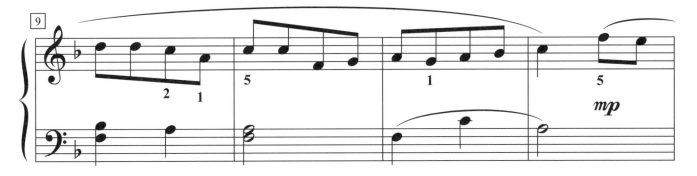

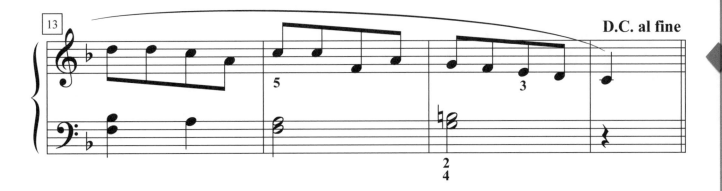

CD Track 5: Performance tempo
CD Track 6: Practice tempo (played twice)

Symphony No. 39

Allegretto ♩ = 126-138

Wolfgang Amadeus Mozart

CD Track 7: Performance tempo
CD Track 8: Practice tempo (played twice)

Mozart (MOE-tsart) is one of the best known composers in the world. During his lifetime of 35 years (1756-1791), he wrote an amazing amount of music. He was a musical genius, who was able to imagine an entire symphony or opera in his mind before writing it down on manuscript paper. In Mozart's time a symphony lasted from 20 to 35 minutes.

Writing a symphony is complicated because the composer must create separate parts for as many as twelve different instruments. Some of the instruments had two parts, for example, 1st violin and 2nd violin. During the summer of 1788, Mozart wrote *three symphonies in three months*, including the one here!

New Boogie

Wesley Schaum

Giocoso ♩= 88-100

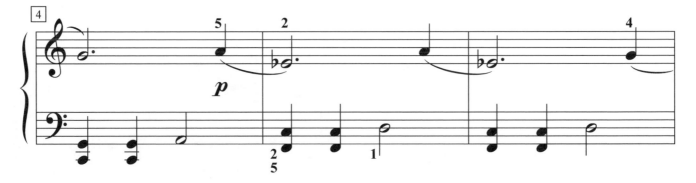

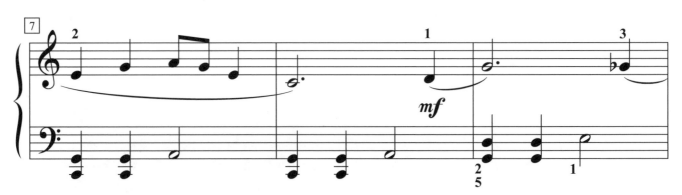

A "blues progression" is a pattern of chords commonly used in blues style music. It is also used in boogie, jazz and rock styles. The blues progression is a 12-measure pattern using chords based on the 1st, 4th and 5th degrees of the scale of the piece. The 12-measure chord sequence is: 1-1-1-1 4-4-1-1 5-4-1-1.

"New Boogie" is written in the key of C major. In the C major scale, the 1st degree is C, the 4th degree is F and the 5th degree is G. These scale degrees are used as the root of the chord in each measure. The first 12 measures of "New Boogie" use the blues progression. The pattern is re-peated in measures 13 through 24.

CD Track 9: Performance tempo
CD Track 10: Practice tempo (played twice)

The excerpt on the next page is Elgar's most famous theme. You will probably recognize it since it is often played at high school graduation ceremonies. It is an orchestral piece written in 1901. In 1911, the same theme was rearranged for the coronation of King Edward VII of England and given the title "Land of Hope and Glory."

During Elgar's visits to the United States, he received an honorary degree from Yale University in 1904, and from the University of Pittsburgh in 1907. He also composed numerous other works for orchestra, chorus, vocal solo and chamber groups.

Duet Accompaniment

CD Track 11: Performance tempo
CD Track 12: Practice tempo (played twice)

Pomp and Circumstance

Maestoso ♩= 72-84

Edward Elgar

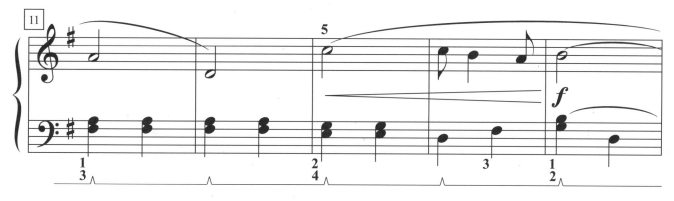

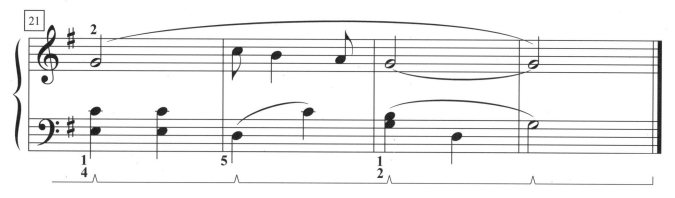

Peacherine Rag

Moderato ♩ = 112-126

Scott Joplin

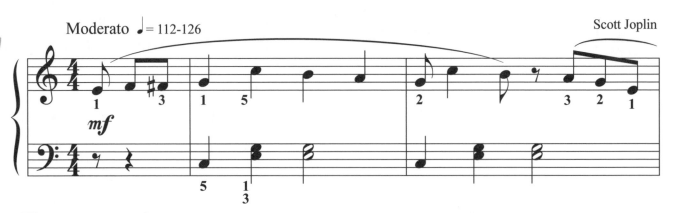

Duet Accompaniment

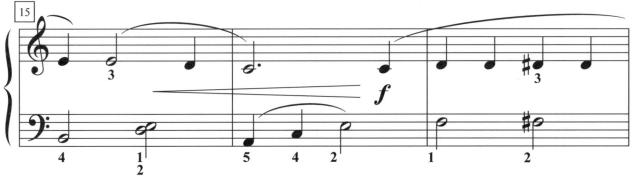

Duet Accompaniment – *continued*

CD Track 13: Performance tempo
CD Track 14: Practice tempo (played twice)

Hallelujah Chorus

Grandioso ♩ = 138-160

George Frederick Handel

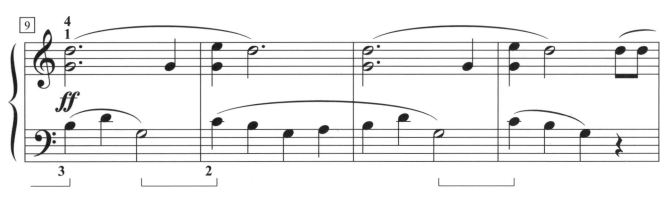

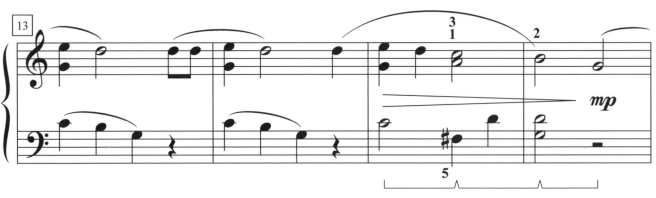

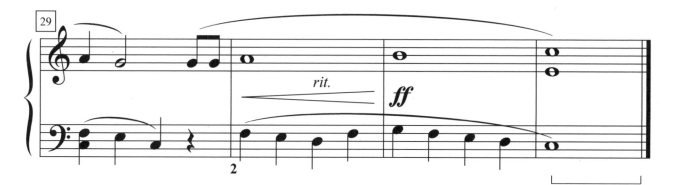

An *oratorio* is a story told with music. It features vocal soloists and choruses accompanied by an orchestra. An oratorio is composed for formal performance in a concert hall.

The "Messiah" is Handel's best known oratorio. The story is based on excerpts from the Bible. It is often performed during the Christmas and Easter seasons. The "Hallelujah Chorus" is the most famous piece from the "Messiah."

George Frederick Handel (HAHN-del) was born in Germany and moved to London, England where he became very famous as a composer. He eventually became a British citizen.

CD Track 15: Performance tempo
CD Track 16: Practice tempo (played twice)

Hail To the Chief

Sir Walter Scott

James Sanderson

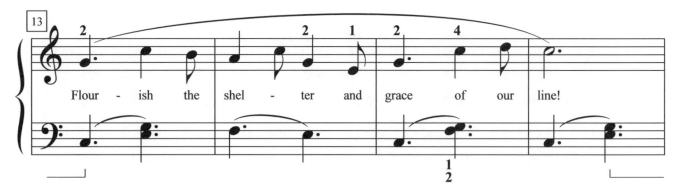

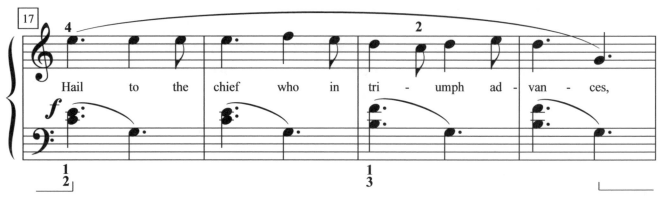

This is the official march of the President of the United States. It is performed by military bands when the president appears for a formal visit or for official ceremonies. It was first played for the inauguration of President James K. Polk in 1845. The music is generally credited to James Sanderson, although there is some doubt about his being the composer. The words are taken from a lengthy poem written by Sir Walter Scott and first published in England about 1810. The poem was originally intended to honor a Scottish chieftan.

CD Track 17: Performance tempo
CD Track 18: Practice tempo (played twice)

On Christmas Eve of 1896, John Philip Sousa was on board a ship crossing the Atlantic Ocean, returning from a vacation in Italy. It was then that he composed the "Stars and Stripes Forever." The march was first performed two days later. Over the years, its popularity has grown and it has become well known all over the world – one of the most famous marches ever written. It was also one of Sousa's personal favorites. In 1987, the U.S. Congress passed a bill which made "Stars and Stripes Forever" the official march of the United States.

Duet Accompaniment

🄭 **CD Track 19: Performance tempo**
CD Track 20: Practice tempo (played twice)

Stars and Stripes Forever

Allegro ♩ = 120-132

John Philip Sousa

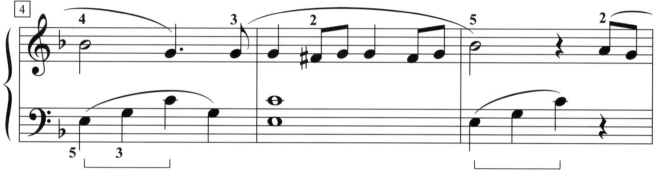

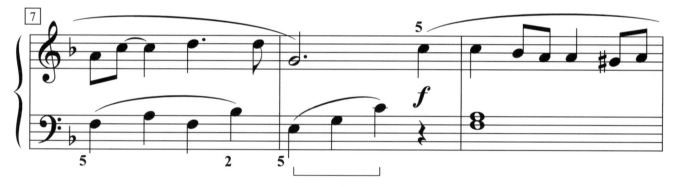

"Sourwood Mountain" is one of the best loved American mountain songs. Because of its popularity, there are many variations both in lyrics and melody. Sourwood is a hardwood tree found in the eastern United States. Sourwood Mountain is in Russell County, Virginia, although the tune is said to be from Kentucky. The music is often played by fiddlers for country dancing. It is a whimsical love song with many nonsense syllables in the lyrics.

Duet Accompaniment

CD Track 21: Performance tempo
CD Track 22: Practice tempo (played twice)

Sourwood Mountain

Animato ♪ = 120-144

American Mountain Tune

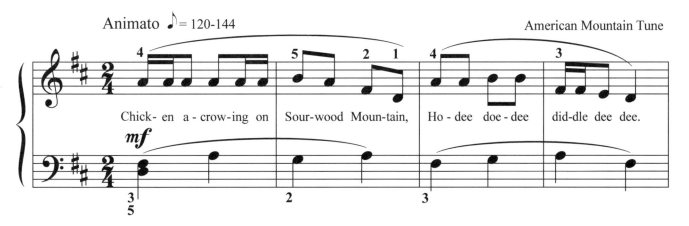

Chick- en a- crow-ing on Sour-wood Moun-tain, Ho - dee doe-dee did-dle dee dee.

So man-y pret-ty girls, I can't count them, Ho - dee doe - dee did-dle dee dee.

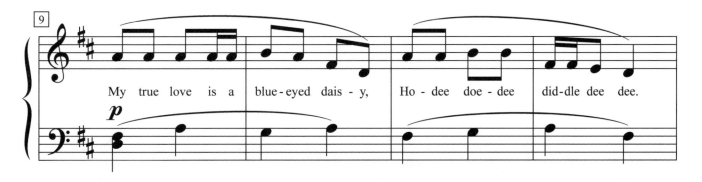

My true love is a blue-eyed dais - y, Ho - dee doe - dee did-dle dee dee.

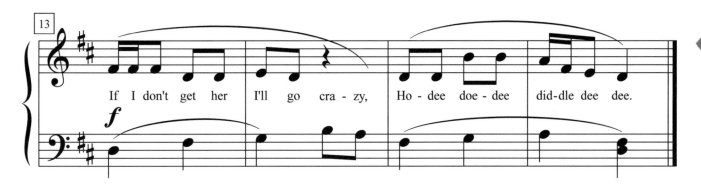

If I don't get her I'll go cra - zy, Ho - dee doe-dee did-dle dee dee.

Semper Fidelis

Vivace ♩. = 100-112

John Philip Sousa

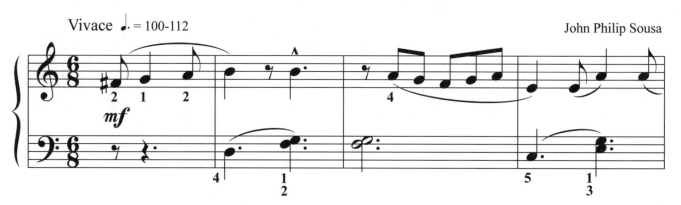

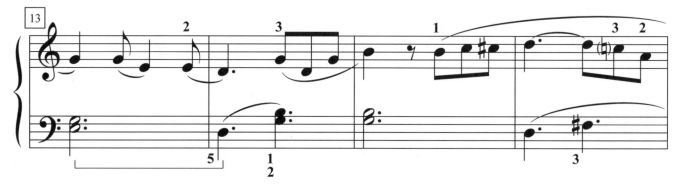

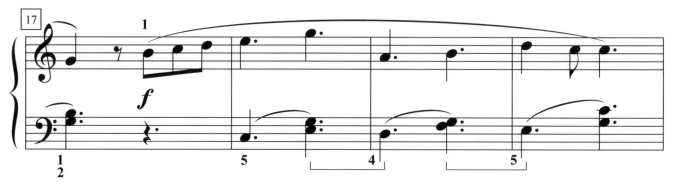

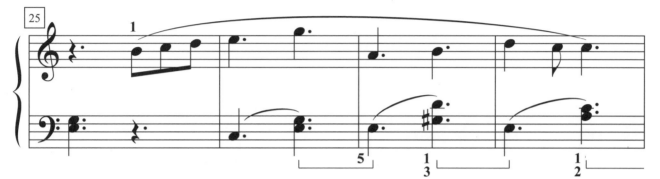

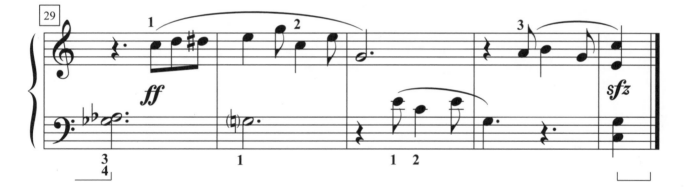

John Philip Sousa was Band Master of the Marine Band when he wrote "Semper Fidelis" in 1888. "Semper Fidelis" ("Always Faithful") is the motto of the U.S. Marines. The band he directed is an elite group of musicians stationed in Washington D.C. This band still performs at the White House and plays for official government ceremonies as well as at regular public concerts. Sousa later formed his own band and toured extensively in the United States, Canada and Europe. The popularity of his compositions earned him the title of "The March King."

CD Track 23: Performance tempo
CD Track 24: Practice tempo (played twice)

Successful Schaum Sheet Music

*= Big Notes   •= Original Form   ✓= Chord Symbols